A FRE

MW01491537

"Money is the tool that makes our dreams come true. In this book, James has given us all a practical, predictable, and understandable way to bring the money we need into our lives."
—Jim Stovall, *New York Times* Bestselling Author of *The Ultimate Gift*

ATTRACT MONEY FOREVER

ATTRACT MONEY FOREVER

A Companion Book to *How to Attract Money Using Mind Power* to Help You Manifest Success and Riches of All Kinds

JAMES GOI JR.

JAMES GOI JR.

JGJ

Attract Money Forever will deepen your understanding of metaphysics and mind-power principles as they relate to attracting money, manifesting abundance, and governing material reality. You'll learn how to use time-tested, time-honored, practical, and spiritual techniques to be more prosperous and improve your life in astounding and meaningful ways. Visit jamesgoijr.com/subscriber-page.html for your free download copy of this amazing book and to receive James's free monthly *Mind Power & Money Ezine*.

THE
GOD
FUNCTION

Books by James Goi Jr.

How to Attract Money Using Mind Power
Attract Money Forever
Ten Metaphysical Secrets of Manifesting Money
Advanced Manifesting Made Easy
Aware Power Functioning
The God Function
The Supernatural Power of Thought
Ten Spiritual Secrets of Dead People
Ten Spiritual Secrets of Divine Order
Ten Spiritual Secrets of Thought Power
Self-Defense Techniques and How to Win a Street Fight
The Healing Power of the Light
Spirituality and Metaphysics
Unconditional Love Demystified
Spiritual Power Demystified
Intuition Demystified
Message from the Presence
The True Nature of Reality
Reincarnation and Karma
Vibration and Frequency
Spiritual Understanding
Spiritual Advancement
Spiritual Knowledge
Spiritual Wisdom
Success Consciousness
Higher Consciousness
Light vs. Darkness
The New Normal
My Song Lyrics (multiple volumes)
JGJ Thoughts, Vol. 1

Note

James continues to write new books.
To see the current list, visit his author page at Amazon.com

THE
GOD
FUNCTION

A Spiritual Journey into Cosmic Consciousness for Attracting
Abundance, Controlling Circumstances, and Manifesting Miracles

JAMES GOI JR.

JGJ
JAMES GOI JR.
LA MESA, CALIFORNIA

ISBN:
978-1-68347-008-3 (Trade Paperback)
978-1-68347-009-0 (Kindle)
978-1-68347-043-4 (epub)

Published by:
James Goi Jr.
P.O. Box 563
La Mesa, CA, 91944
www.jamesgoijr.com

CONTENTS

Preface

PREFACE

This is one of three books I wrote in 2010-2011 that sprang forth spontaneously when I sat down to write something much shorter and unrelated. After a few days, and just a few writing sessions, I had this book. (The other two books are *Advanced Manifesting Made Easy* and *Aware Power Functioning*.)

I had the distinct feeling while writing that the book had already been written somewhere else and that I was just putting it down on paper to bring it into the here and now. Other writers have talked of similar types of processes and experiences.

The book was not planned out or outlined, as is more or less standard practice in the writing of nonfiction books such as this, but instead was just written from one end to the other. In preparation for publishing this book, I separated it into titled chapters, did some editing and cleaning up, and the result is the book you now hold in your hands.

Before you go any further, I want to tell you this: You do not have to work this God Function angle if you're not comfortable with it or would just rather not for some reason. It's one way of getting much of what you want and need from the universe. It's a powerful way. It's an effective way. But it's not the only way. If you want to do it, if you want to use this method, then good. And if you don't want to do it, then that's good too. There are many ways of doing things. There are many ways of looking at things.

Follow this path if you want to. See where it leads you. See if you believe yourself better off for having engaged in the process. And know, too, that this way of working with the universe can be done in harmony with other methods and systems you might now be using or might take up in the future.

You are in control here. Only you can know what is best for you and what is right for you. Be true to yourself on this journey through your life and on this path to higher understanding and increased spiritual knowledge, and everything will always work out for the best in the end.

To get the best results from reading this book, I recommend that you read it as I believe it was intended to be read—in one sitting.

Do that, and I believe the person who gets up from that chair will not be the same person who sat down in it. And I believe the life you enter upon rising will not be the same life you exited when you started reading. Some books have the very real power to change lives. I believe this is one of those books.

THE GOD FUNCTION

1
It Doesn't Matter

Does God exist? That question could be pondered, discussed, and debated without end. And what would be the outcome of all that pondering, discussion, and debate? Same as it's always been: Some people would believe God exists, and some people would believe God does not exist.

If God *does* exist, then what *is* God? That question could be pondered, discussed, and debated without end. And what would be the outcome of all that pondering, discussion, and debate? Same as it's always been: Some people would believe God is an individual being, and some people would believe God is all things, including all people.

So, does God exist or not exist? This is a fair question, but for the purposes of this book the answer doesn't matter. So, if God *does* exist, then what *is* God? This is a fair question, but for the purposes of this book the answer doesn't matter.

The reason it doesn't matter whether or not God exists will be revealed to you in just a moment. The reason it doesn't matter what God is will be revealed to you in just a moment.

What do you want out of life? Better health? Better relationships? More worldly success? More opportunities for self-expression and sharing? Financial security? Peace of mind? To be safe? What do you want out of life? Think about it.

You can have many of the things you want out of life, and likely to a degree you haven't yet imagined. And just how are you to go about the task of attaining many of the things you want out of life? The answer will be revealed to you in just a moment.

First, here's the reason it doesn't matter whether or not God exists: It doesn't matter whether or not God exists because the God Function *does* exist. And here's the reason it doesn't matter what God is: It doesn't matter what God is because you can know what the God Function is.

And now for the answer to how you can have many of the things you want out of life: You can have many of the things you want out of life because you can learn to use the God Function to get them.

You can ponder, discuss, and debate whether or not God exists if you like. You can ponder, discuss, and debate what God is if you like. Perhaps all your pondering, discussing, and debating will help you to get clearer about whether or not God exists and about what God is. But then again, perhaps all your pondering, discussing, and debating will cause you to become more confused about whether or not God exists and about what God is.

You might end up with opinions you mistake for knowledge. You might end up with genuine knowledge. You could spend years pondering, discussing, and debating the existence and nature of God. Indeed, many do. You could spend most of your life pondering, discussing, and debating the existence and nature of God. Indeed, many have.

And in the meantime, there are experiences you want to have, things you want to do, and expenses you have to pay. Whether or not your pondering, discussing, and debating will help you with those practical matters is, well, a question that could be pondered, discussed, and debated without end.

Understand that this book is not about whether or not God exists. Understand that this book is not about what God is. This book is about the God Function. This book is about how you can use the God Function to cause your circumstances to be what you want them to be. You can be supplied, successful, and safe. You can be happy, healthy, and helpful. You can be prosperous, prolific, and at peace.

You are about to learn what the God Function is. You are about to learn how the God Function works. You are about to learn how to work the God Function. You are about to learn how to live an inspired, charmed, and magical life.

2
It's a Mechanism

The God Function can give you everything you need. In fact, the God Function knows better than you what you need. The God Function can give you much of what you want. In fact, the God Function knows better than you what you want. This might all sound too good to be true. It's not. And once you know what the God Function is, you'll understand why it's not.

So, what exactly *is* the God Function? The God Function is a mechanism existing within the very fabric of creation that acts as God is generally said and thought to act. That's it. Here it is again: *The God Function is a mechanism existing within the very fabric of creation that acts as God is generally said and thought to act.*

Whereas one could credibly argue that God does not exist, one could not do so concerning the God Function. Any fair- and open-minded person understanding the facts would likely conclude that, whether or not God exists, there is certainly some sort of mechanism in the universe that acts as God is generally said and thought to act.

If you are a fair- and open-minded person, you will benefit greatly from reading this book. This book was not written to convince you of anything. If you are a skeptic, you might well still be one when you get to the last page. This book is instructional in nature. It teaches how the God Function works and how people can think and act in ways that will best help them benefit from the action of the God Function.

The God Function is as basic as it is profound. The God Function is as simple as it is sensational. People have been reporting and describing the actions of this mechanism throughout human history. Religions have been built upon these reports and descriptions. Countless books have been written about various aspects of the God Function.

Some people have spent their entire lives trying to educate people on the nature and workings of the God Function, regardless of what they called it or thought it was. It is human nature to make things more complex than they need to be. It is human nature to miss the point. It is human nature to go off on mental tangents and to never return, making those tangents no longer tangents but the very substance and nature of an individual's life.

But some people can see the simplicity of Truth. Some people can get the point. Some people can stay on a chosen path without being unduly distracted or misdirected. This book was written for such people.

On some level, you have seen and recognized the God Function at work in your life and in the lives of others. The truth of the God Function is self-evident. It needs no defending. The God Function exists. The God Function is predictable. The God Function is dependable. The God Function works.

Your life will be transformed to the degree you accept the validity of the God Function, invite it into your experience, and act in ways harmonious with how the God Function acts. This is not a complex process, so don't make it one. Just clear your mind, get informed, and then move decisively in the direction you want to go.

Whether or not God exists is not your concern at this time. What God might be is not your concern at this time. The God Function has been described here as a mechanism that acts as God is generally said and thought to act. To govern the action of the God Function, act as if God exists and in a way that will help you to get what you want and need.

This could not be much simpler: There is a mechanism in creation that acts as God is generally said and thought to act, and your job is to act as if that mechanism is God Itself and in a way that will help you have what you deem a good life.

You already know most of what you need to know in that you know how God is generally said and thought to act. It is up to you now to do more of what you need to do, which is to nurture and expand your relationship with your concept of God and your working connection with the God Function.

If you are a more metaphysically minded person, you might have a concept of God as being and including all things. Even for you, this is good advice: In part, at least, treat the concept of God as if God is an individual, conscious being.

3
The Concept of God

Why treat the concept of God as if God is an individual, conscious being? Because doing so seems to be the easiest and most effective way for the average person to interact with the God Function.

Consider these suggestions: God is said and thought to be the Father, so approach God as His child. God is said and thought to be all-seeing, so strive to act as if you know God is watching you. God is said and thought to be all-knowing, so strive to think and feel as if you know God knows your thoughts and feelings. God is said and thought to answer prayers, so pray to God. God is said and thought to punish bad deeds, so avoid doing them. God is said and thought to reward good deeds, so strive to do them.

Consider this suggestion: Regardless of what your concept of God has been up to this point, and even if up until now you believed God to be the impersonal totality of all that is, sincerely work at nurturing the concept of God as an individual, conscious being that is aware of your existence and circumstances and that cares about you.

You might think yours has been an advanced concept of God, and perhaps it has been. But you should not be as concerned with the concept or theory of God as you should be with the reality and applicability of the God Function and how you can best interact with it to get what you want and need in this life.

Now, it might well be that it is an expansion of consciousness to widen one's concept of what God is, but an unintended and undesirable consequence of doing so can be a decrease in the God Function's direct and desired action in one's life.

To some people a larger God represents more freedom and personal power for the individual but since human beings tend to be weak, selfish, and unfocused in some fundamental ways many are just not in a position to prudently and effectively handle that increase in freedom and personal power. Think about how humanity has handled the increase of freedom and personal power it has gained through the use of its advancing technology.

The more expanded version of God often leaves the welfare of the individual in his or her own hands, and—for many people—therein lies the problem. Sure, it would be nice if all human beings were capable of successfully running their own lives. But of course, all human beings are not.

If up to this time you *have* thought of God in the tra-
ditional sense, as an individual entity, you would do
well to begin to include aspects of the more expanded version of God within your concept. Think about
it. Why limit God? Why does God have to be either
personal or impersonal? If there is a God, it is likely
that the very nature of this God is unlimited in all
ways fundamental and practical. So, think: Why can't
God be both a personal *and* an impersonal being?

If you subscribe to the more expanded version of
God as all things everywhere, then you believe each
individual human being is, in effect, God. And it fol-
lows that many of these people, who are in effect God
Itself, would believe in a personal God—one above,
beyond, and outside them. But if they are unknow-
ingly God themselves, with the powers and abilities
they attribute to God, their belief in a personal God
could—in theory, at least—*create* a personal God
even if before one did not exist.

Assuming there is a God and that It started out impersonal and universal, It might have been modified
or adjusted by having been condensed by individualizations of Itself—and one must wonder how those
individualizations even came about to begin with—
into some all-powerful supreme Individualization
Itself. Individual individualizations of God may have
increased their governing power over the impersonal

overriding God by introducing this pivotal new attribute into it: Individualization. A God on a throne. And so, in effect, an *individual.*

Assuming there is a God, It just might be at the same time so much more and so much less than human beings have ever dreamed It to be.

How can human beings accurately judge the nature and scope of God? The answer is that human beings cannot accurately judge the nature and scope of God. Human beings functioning from the human perspective are limited and, therefore, not fit to judge something that at Its core and in the end is quite likely *unlimited.* Human beings cannot even *know* beyond doubt that "God" exists in any form even remotely resembling their concept of It—and thinking they can do so might just be the height of human ignorance, arrogance, and absurdity.

4
The God that Functions

Theorizing about God can be a mental, emotional, and even spiritual experience, the result of which can be opinion, belief, and even knowledge. Ask a group of people what God is, and it's not likely any two will give the same exact answer. Your concern should not be so much what God is as what you *think* God is.

You are, in effect, determining what you want to think God is so that God will act as if It is that. And you want to have a concept of God that is highly supportive of your personal interests and wellbeing. It might start out as an exercise of the mind, but it should progress to being a condition of the heart.

In other words, you want to absorb your chosen concept of God into the very fiber of your being. You should accept your concept of God as being an accurate concept because it is accurate, not because you want to materially gain from having it.

An effective way to proceed is to think not first of the God Function but of the God that functions. You'll in practice interact with God so that you can in effect interact with the God Function. Think about it. Would the average person be more enthusiastic about praying to and depending on an all-powerful Supreme Being or an impersonal, indifferent mechanism within the universe at large?

You want to have an ongoing working relationship with the God Function so you can get what you want and need from the universe, and an effective way to do that is to have an ongoing personal relationship with what you deem to be God.

Again, your concern should not be what God is but what you *think* God is. And God will act as if It is what you think It is. You must go beyond your concept of God into the very depths of the God Function, which in essence *is* God, even if an impersonal mechanism is all that exists.

You must bring yourself to fully believe your chosen concept of God accurately reflects the reality of God. Otherwise you will not be interacting with God, you will be interacting with your personal concept of God and, therefore, with your limited self.

Within the makeup of the universal structure is the God Function mechanism. It is observable through its actions, which are observable through those action's effects. The God Function acts, and you as a human being are acted upon by the God Function. To make it more likely that the God Function will continue to act upon you in ways you would choose it to, choose to believe in a God behind the function.

You might not be able to know God in a way you would deem absolute and indisputable, but you can certainly know the God Function in a way that is obvious and undeniable. The source of the function is of course open to interpretation, but the function itself can be known for what it is.

Throughout human history God has been pondered while the God Function has been recorded. God has been the subject of imagination while the God Function has been the subject of observation. God does not lend Itself well to assessment, but the God Function can be studied and comprehended. God might be outside the individual's direct control, but the God Function can be governed by the individual for his or her own benefit, and thus the individual can control the *activity* of God—although indirectly.

To govern the God Function so it brings about the positive outcomes you desire, you must simply understand how the God Function operates and then adjust your own thoughts, feelings, and actions so they cause the God Function to react in ways you have decided will benefit you. It's a miraculous and wondrous process, and the key to its operation is firmly in your hand. And in this book, you are being given one way to turn that key.

So if you do in fact want to turn this key, from here on out begin to move away from the idea of a concept of God to the idea of a God Itself. Believe in God. Turn to God. Whatever God is, if anything, is a moot point. Whatever God does, which is everything, is the whole point. And what God does can only be known by observing God's function: The God Function.

5
Harmonious Alignment

The God Function is the mechanism within the universe that reflects back to you the nature and substance of what you are.

The consciousness behind the God Function—as demonstrated by its actions—is clearly good. To move into harmonious alignment with the God Function, you be good too.

The consciousness behind the God Function—as demonstrated by its actions—is clearly benevolent. To move into harmonious alignment with the God Function, you be benevolent too.

The consciousness behind the God Function—as demonstrated by its actions—is clearly loving. To move into harmonious alignment with the God Function, you be loving too.

What you think and how you feel are the true measures of what you are. Anyone can act in ways inconsistent with the truth of how they think and feel. But how people think and feel is how they *are* at their core. Know that God knows you for what you are. You cannot fool God. God knows your heart.

To cause the God Function to work for your benefit, purify your very essence. Cleanse the substance of what you are of anything coarse and ugly. Such energy repels the positive operation of the God Function. Study your heart. Be honest with yourself about what you have become and what you now are.

Without self-honesty, there is no solid foundation for a positive connection to the God Function or a positive relationship with God. You want to know and acknowledge the truth about yourself. You want to improve in the areas that need improving.

If you have negative feelings toward other people or dissatisfaction with God because you are not happy with your present circumstances, or if you wish inharmonious conditions upon any person, you are effectively slamming the door in God's face and putting a barrier between you and the positive action of the God Function in your life.

To be harmoniously aligned with God and with the God Function (collectively "the God Force"), you must be aligned in expression and intent. The expression and intent of the God Force are always positive, loving, and helpful. Are you?

One of the most effective ways of attracting harmonious circumstances and repelling inharmonious circumstances is to continually express an energy and consciousness of love, goodwill, tolerance, understanding, and kindness.

The God Force recognizes Its own and Itself wherever Its own and Itself are expressing. Think and act as the God Force thinks and acts, and you become the God Force. To the extent you think and act not only *as* the God Force but *for* the God Force, you effectively *are* the God Force. You effectively are *God*.

It is the nature of God that no bad thing can befall It. It is the nature of God that no harm can come to It. It is the nature of God that nothing is more powerful than It. And it is the nature of God to recognize, absorb, and enfold all that is like Itself. Understand this great truth: To the extent that you are recognized, absorbed, and enfolded by God, you too, like God, will be above bad things and harm and, like God, there will be nothing more powerful than you.

To take on or assume the power of God to a greater degree than you might already be doing, simply act in Godlike ways more than you've been doing. Do this first in thought and feeling, and it will naturally follow that you will do this in tangible, outward ways. Remember, you can't fool God. Remember,

God is watching. And know that God breathes life into you just as you have breathed life into God.

You can know the heart of God by allowing it to be reflected into your own heart. And you can know the actions of God by observing the miraculous circumstances and events unfolding upon the surface of your daily life. You will see and know that the God Function will become one with the circumstances and events of your daily life to the degree you become one with the heart and mind of God.

As a human being, you are inherently frail and vulnerable in some fundamental ways. With the God Function on your side, though, you can rise above many of your weaknesses and limitations.

6
Days with God

To do well at governing the operation of the God Function, know God. God should be real for you. You would do well to make God a central focal point of your consciousness on an ongoing daily basis. Reach for God, and It will lift you up. Trust God, and It will be worthy of your trust. Rely on God, and you will be cared for and watched over.

You want your relationship with God to be as close as your relationship with yourself. And as you go through your daily routine, you can have this over-riding thought process running in the background: Who is acting here? Me? Or God?

If you want God to act *for* you, then you would do well to allow God to act *through* you. Whether you know it or not, whether you recognize it in any particular situation or not, God is always attempting to move your mind, heart, soul, and body. Allow God to move you. Allow yourself to be moved.

And consider including God among your first thoughts each day. For instance, acknowledge God.

Greet God. If you want the God Function to work at a high level on your behalf during the upcoming day, then you will do well to interact with God when you are first starting your day.

Once you have gotten your day off to a divine start by acknowledging and greeting the presence of God, you would do well to acknowledge some of what God has done for you and is doing for you. Sincere gratitude for what God does for you can be a magic elixir that solidifies and strengthens the relationship between you and God and the working connection between you and the God Function.

Think about how the God Function has been operating in your life in both the recent and distant past. You don't have to spend a lot of time in this process. The nature and sincerity of a gratitude session are much more important than the duration of a gratitude session. Expressing gratitude for even just a few moments will have a profound effect.

Once you have given what you deem sufficient time and attention to gratitude on a given morning, now that you have acknowledged that God is present and have thanked God for Its ongoing assistance, it's time to move on to the next step. At this point, you would do well to tell God what you want and need and to ask God to assist you in getting those things.

Believe that God wants to help you. Believe that God wants to give you what you want and need. And the best way you can help God to help you and to give you what you want and need is to tell God what you want and need and to ask God for what you want and need. This practice is commonly called *prayer*.

Prayer is an effective method of setting the God Function to work at bringing into your life those specific circumstances and things you have decided you want. Prayer is also an effective method of setting the God Function to work at watching over and protecting you and those you include in your prayers. More than simply an antiquated religious ritual, prayer is a timeless and powerful metaphysical technique for interacting with the mind of God, with the mind of the universe, in an active, focused way.

And although prayer is an active process in a fundamental way, it is also a passive process in a fundamental way. It is an active process in that you are taking the initiative to ask God for what you want and need, and it is a passive process in that you are giving over to God the responsibility to get done what needs to be done on Its part. You are effectively giving the job of fulfillment to God.

Of course, you might have to do some things to get what you want in any particular situation. Those things will be shown to you in due time, and you will have divine assistance while doing them. But again, you are effectively giving the job of fulfillment to God. You are recognizing God as the power and intelligence behind the positive circumstances that arise in your life. And by so doing, you are *causing* God to be the power and intelligence behind the positive circumstances that arise in your life.

In other words, if it wasn't already true—that God is the power and intelligence behind the positive circumstances in your life—it will be true now, even if you are the one at the very bottom of it all.

7
Live Your Life Right

Believe that God *is* the power and intelligence behind the positive circumstances that arise in your life. And believing this, it will be natural for you to trust that God will do what needs to be done so that all things line up to allow the fruits of your intentions to spring forth into material reality.

So again, pray for what you need. Pray for what you want. And be confident that your prayers will be answered, and think as big as you feel inclined to think. God's ability to answer your prayers is limited mainly by your prayers themselves and your belief that God can, will, and has answered them.

That's right, *has* answered them. In the timeless mind of God, your prayers have been answered even before they've been answered. In the timeless mind of God, your prayers have been answered even before they've been made. Still, you can do no more powerful a thing than to pray for what you want and need in a spirit of belief that what you ask will be and has been done. And do this in a spirit of *gratitude* for the fact that what you ask will be and has been done.

And of course, prayer is not only for the mornings just as breathing is not only for the mornings. Ideally, prayer should be an ongoing and consistent process running alongside all your other habitual mental and emotional processes.

If you want to enlist the significant and ongoing help of the God Function, you must live your life right. In order to live your life right, you must live your days right. In order to live your days right, you must *start* your days right. And to help yourself start your days right, you can do no more powerful a thing than to start your days off with God.

And again, how do you do that? You do that by, first thing each day, opening your eyes to God. You do that by opening your heart to God. You do that by knowing God and by allowing God to know you.

First thing each day, acknowledge God, express gratitude to God, and pray to God. Then, throughout each day, acknowledge some more, express gratitude some more, and pray some more. And again, these actions do not have to take a lot of time. A little can go a long way when it's done in the *right* way.

Above and beyond separate mental actions and activities each day, your overall consciousness and frame of mind will set the spiritual tone for your life. You want the spiritual tone of your life to be of such a nature as to cause you to come into intimate and harmonious alignment with God and with the God Function (again, collectively, "the God Force").

Always remember, at the bottom of everything you are reading about here, there is *consciousness*. Consciousness moves matter. Consciousness moves the world. Consciousness is force. There are varying kinds and degrees of force.

For instance, there is malevolent force by which individuals through ill will or action wish upon or deliver upon others evil and harm, even if there is no direct, tangible gain to be had by doing so.

A step up, you find selfish force by which human beings attempt to sway events in such ways as to bring them gain in ways that might cause loss to others.

Up a bit further, there is misguided force by which confused or careless individuals cause harm, loss, or disharmony to others not by design but by misunderstanding or indifference.

Then there is well-intentioned force, which is meant to be helpful and supportive of others and often is. But of course, well-intentioned force is sometimes also misguided force and can have negative effects.

And then there is spiritual force—the God Force. The God Force is divine in nature and thus all of its actions are in divine harmony. The God Force always works toward the highest best good of all concerned, and never causes one person to gain by causing undue loss to another person.

Keep in mind that any force tends to affect that at which it is directed. Negative force tends to have negative effects, and positive force tends to have positive affects. And often one cannot accurately judge whether a certain force and its resulting effects were negative or positive, as there is too much confusion in human minds and too much deceit and misdirection between human minds to *allow* there to be consistently accurate judgment.

Again, consciousness moves matter. Consciousness moves the world. Consciousness is force. There are varying kinds and degrees of force.

One key to living your life right is to intelligently moderate your use of force.

8
God's Instrument

So that you may help keep yourself harmoniously aligned with God and with the God Function, follow these simple rules: never knowingly and purposely exert malevolent force; never knowingly and purposely exert selfish force; strive to not exert misguided force; strive to exert well-intentioned force; strive to allow spiritual force—the God Force—to be exerted through you and upon you.

There will be times that the nature of the force applied will be exposed and made apparent by the effects upon that on which the force has been applied. And at other times the nature of the force applied will be beyond accurate assessment. Things are not always what they seem, and human judgment is inconsistent and less than optimal.

And keep in mind that, in line with how consciousness flows through the universe, exerted force does not only affect that upon which the force is applied. Exerted force also affects that which exerted the force. This important point bears repeating: *Exerted force also affects that which exerted the force.*

So, regarding human-initiated force: malevolent force returns to the originator of malevolent force; selfish force returns to the originator of selfish force; misguided force returns to the originator of misguided force; and well-intentioned force returns to the originator of well-intentioned force. Knowing this, you should see that it makes good sense to never knowingly and purposely exert any nature of force you do not want to be exerted upon you.

The practical and significant implications of having force return to you are that the force will tend to have upon you the same type of effect it was intended to have upon, or did have upon, those it was directed at. You should be able to see the wisdom in the practice of never wishing upon another person anything you would not wish upon yourself.

As for spiritual force, the God Force, it works in much the same way that human-initiated force works. It returns to that consciousness (in this case, God) that exerted it. Thus, God would appear to always be strengthening Itself (if that is possible) or at the very least maintaining Its strength by the fact that there is a closed loop of high-powered spiritual energy constantly going out from and returning to God. The will and intent of God is expressed from the mind of God through the medium of the God Function and thus is expressed as the God Force.

And you, as a recipient of the God Force through the action of the God Function, receive the great benefit of God's will and intent for you—which, if you are an active participant in the process, will, in part, have been previously chosen by you and/or agreed upon by you. God acts through the God Function, and you, in effect, get to tell God what to do.

Remember, too, that God not only acts *upon* you but also *through* you. God thus makes you an instrument through which It does Its work. So much of the good that can come upon any person must in one way or another, directly or indirectly, come from or through other people. Position yourself to be one of those people through which God can act upon others.

Not only will doing so help you to repay your great and ongoing debt to God, but doing so will greatly increase the positive benefits you receive in your life as a result of your relationship with God.

Understand that when God works through you by putting you in between the God Function and another person—basically and in effect channeling God's will, intent, and action through you—for practical purposes it is as if *you* were the consciousness that exerted the resultant God Force and action. You will be the vessel through which God's will is done, but you will benefit as if *you* are God Itself.

If you act as an instrument through which God can touch the lives of other people, you allow the God Force to pass through you and onto those other people. You already know that all the positive energy extended from the mind of God must return to God, but what you might not have recognized is that if you acted as an instrument of that energy, it must pass through you on its way back to God.

9
God Personified

When you act for and on behalf of God in material ways (say, by giving money to someone in need) and non-material ways (say, by expressing unconditional love), you have, in effect: made God's energy your energy; made God's will your will; and made God's action your action. And you have, in effect and in the moment, become one with God. For practical purposes, you have become God Personified.

Know that the more closely aligned you are with God, the more the line separating you and God blurs. Really think about that. God can be seen indirectly through the action of the God Function, and when you are an instrument through which the God Function operates, God can be seen *through you*. God can be seen *in you*. Your face becomes the face of God. In effect, in that moment, you *are* God.

To benefit the most from the action of the God Function, you will do well to cultivate as close a relationship with God as possible. And one very effective way to do that important task is to become a personification of God. And you do *this* by becoming

33

an instrument through which the God Function can act upon the lives of other human beings.

Remember, much of the good that can come to any human being must, in one way or another, directly or indirectly, come from or through other people. Of course, much of the good that can come to any human being can come directly to that person from God/the God Function/the God Force.

Such things as spiritual healing of the mind, heart, and soul of an individual often do not need the aid of a human intermediary. And such things as increased spiritual strength, clarity, and enlightenment often do not need a human intermediary.

Still, the fact remains that much of the good that can come to any human being must, in one way or another, directly or indirectly, come from or through other people. Even such things as spiritual healing and enlightenment can be helped along by human intermediaries acting as bridges between God and humans. Two examples: a person can say something another person needs to hear, and a person can lead someone to a book that second person needs to read.

And, of course, it should be clearly evident that when it comes to the day-to-day things and circumstances of material life such as money, jobs, opportunities, information, and so on, human intermediaries are almost always a part of the process of bringing these things and a given person together.

Again, you want to position yourself in such a way as to be one of those people through which God can easily act upon others. How you do that is by paying attention to what is going on around you and to your inner feelings and inclinations having to do with what is going on around you.

When you work for God you are always on duty, or more accurately perhaps, you are always on call. People need God's help in their lives and you should be a willing and available instrument God can use to get that help to those people. So you may consistently do this job at a high level of proficiency, you must be ever alert. And you must sincerely strive to never let one opportunity to serve God get away from you.

And so much of what you will be called upon to do will be relatively easy and painless for you to do. Sometimes God just wants to smile at someone. God needs a human being to pass that smile along. Sometimes God wants to give encouragement to someone. God often needs a person to pass that encouragement along. Sometimes God wants to give comfort and assurance to someone. God often needs a person—like you for instance—to pass them along.

Remember, nothing God ever does is insignificant—no matter how seemingly small it is. There is a reason for everything God does, and the reason is always important. Do you realize how much an encouraging word from you can mean to someone who hasn't heard an encouraging word in months and who is on the verge of giving up hope?

Do you realize that a smile from you and a radiation of true unconditional love can give a person two hours away from suicide the strength to go on for another day? That person might have long ago closed themselves off from being able to feel God's love directly, but they will certainly feel it through you if you let it flow as freely as you are able to do. And God's love can help to heal that person. Do you have any idea at all of how big a role you can play in healing the planet, one heart at a time?

10
Your Natural Flow

No, you likely do not have any true concept of how big a role you can play in healing the planet one heart at a time. How could you? But God has the concept. And that's all you need to know.

There's nothing for you to figure out. There's nothing for you to plan on other than simply being aware of the process of being a channel for God's love, will, and action, being open to the process, and being on the lookout for opportunities to participate in it. The rest will just naturally flow as you allow it to.

It's the same process regarding your own life. Just as God wants to share Its love, will, and action with other people in the world, God wants to share Its love, will, and action with you. The difference between you and the average person is that you get to consciously, intentionally, and knowingly participate in the process of deciding what God's love, will, and action will look like in your life.

Understand that when you become one with God, God's will becomes your will. Understand that God wants for you what you want for yourself. God wants you to explore the possibilities of what you can be, and God knows the best way It can do that is to allow you the space and ability to express your free will in thought and deed. In this way, God helps you become more of what you can be, and in the process, God becomes more of what It can be through you.

This is the agreement: you listen to God, and God will listen to you; you hear God, and God will hear you; you follow God's direction, and God will follow your direction. And the key ingredient that makes this relationship work is *harmony*.

Harmonious conditions can be defined as conditions of agreement and accord. And harmonious conditions are conditions that are consistent and orderly. Where there is harmony, there is a pleasant interaction or arranging of various parts.

So, you want to be in agreement and accord with God in all ways to the best of your ability, you want to be consistent and orderly in this process, and you want your interaction with God to be natural and pleasant.

This process being described *is* a *natural* process. It's the most natural process in the world. It's how things were designed to be. This is in stark contrast to the relationship the average person has with God.

The average person on this planet is not aware of the presence of God, and this lack of clear and accurate perception causes a discordant, low vibration atmosphere to form around the person.

Again, you are seeking to establish a harmonious relationship with God. And how do you do that? You do that by consistently listening for, hearing, and acting upon the voice of God. And how will you *know* which voice is God? You will know through the ongoing practice and experience of being open to intuition, inspiration, and spiritual guidance.

Intuition can be defined, in part, as that deep knowing within you that some fact is true, that things are a certain way, even though you did not come to this knowing through the normal means of accessing information from your environment and then forming conclusions based on that information.

Inspiration can be defined, in part, as a divine influence upon your thoughts and feelings that will often prompt you to, and incline you to, act in certain ways that will clearly represent and express the consciousness behind the inspiration.

And *spiritual guidance* can be defined, in part, as the natural flow and blending of intuition and inspiration as they relate to an individual.

Through intuition you will know what you need to know, and through inspiration you will feel what you need to do and how you should do it. And through sincere effort and cooperation on your part, you will act on what you know and in those ways you are divinely prompted to act.

This process might sound difficult to you, but it's not really difficult at all. What you are doing now is difficult because, to some degree, you are fighting God. But when you get into your natural flow with God, you will finally be able to stop fighting.

11
God's Influence

You are endeavoring to create the overall climate in which the God Function can and will consistently act in your life in the ways you choose it to act. But this doesn't mean you want to choose all of your circumstances by conscious reasoning and choice.

Know that God has a plan for you. You know some of that plan through certain of your longings and aspirations, but you don't know and can't know the whole plan. And certain aspects of the plan would be surprising to you because they concern things you never considered doing and having, things you never knew you wanted to do or have.

And know that some aspects of your own plan for your life might end up being things that are not right for you and that do not end up coming to fruition. So, although you want to be self-directed to a considerable degree, you also want to remain flexible regarding what comes about in your life.

To the extent that you are able to realize significant portions of God's plan for you in this lifetime, you will be pleasantly surprised by the fact that God really does know better than you what you want and really does know better than you what you need.

Can you believe that? Can you bring yourself to believe that, just as you have brought yourself to believe in the God in question? You must believe it so you can create the conditions in which it can be true.

And speaking of the God in question: The God in question should not *be* in question as far as you are concerned. Understand that if you want God to act like God, and if you want to recognize when God *does* act like God, you must *believe* in God.

The God Function Itself exists. That is an observable fact. The existence of the God behind the God Function—if that God is there—can be and is often called into question. It's often debated and doubted.

But don't you debate. Don't you doubt. Every human being has the right to believe about God what they feel inclined to believe, and that's their business. That's their process. That's their experience. Let other people debate with them. You have nothing to debate because you have no doubt. You don't need to try to convince others in a masked attempt to try to convince yourself. You are free of all that. You already know what you need to know.

And just what is it you need to know? You need to know that: God exists; God is aware of you; God wants only good for you; and God will, through the medium of the God Function, deliver into your life those good things you can conceive of and accept and some great things you haven't conceived of.

And strive to remain in the awareness that God exists and acts in your life in both large and small ways. There is no area of your life that is not important to God. God wants you to live the best life you are capable of living. God wants you to be the best you that you are capable of being.

Through the processes of intuition, inspiration, and spiritual guidance, God will help you think, feel, and act in ways consistent with you living the best life you can live and being the best you that you can be. This influence can be felt *and known* by you if you are receptive to it in the various areas of your life.

God's influence can be there, helping you think, feel, and act in ways that empower you to be more and to do more. God's influence will cause you to be patient when you might have otherwise been short-tempered. God's influence will cause you to make good dietary choices when you otherwise might have made choices not in harmony with maintaining your physical health. God's influence will cause you to make good financial decisions when you otherwise might have made decisions that would cause you financial loss.

In these ways and so many others, through intuition, inspiration, and spiritual guidance, God will lift you into a life and a you that on your own you could never have attained. In ways small and large, near and far, God will cause Its presence to be a foundational part of your human experience.

12
Divine Intervention

So much of God's influence on your life will be on *you*. God will touch you directly, causing you to think, feel, and act in ways most conducive to you living the best life you can live and you being the best you that you can be. And God can touch you in other ways such as by healing illness. Such a process can be called *divine intervention*.

Much of God's influence on your life will not be on you directly but, instead, will be on circumstances, conditions, events, and other people. God will, in ways large and small, intervene on your behalf.

This process can also be referred to as *divine intervention*. It is a process through which God will, on your behalf, intervene in the affairs of the world in ways that will help bring about those things God wants to help bring about for you. And if you have developed and nurtured your personal relationship with God and your working relationship with the God Function, much of what God will want to bring about for you will be things you have previously determined you want to come about in your life.

As you become accustomed to this spiritual way of life—which, of course, is what it is—you will be able to sense more and more that there is a presence that goes before you. This presence knows where you will be days, weeks, and years before you get there. This presence knows what you will face before you face it, and It has already supplied what you need so you can benefit in the various ways you need to benefit.

The more you become aware of this process taking place in your life, the more you will have the feeling of being in a story that has already been written and in which you are simply playing your part. You will feel a growing sense of peace that all is well and will continue to be well. Divine order will be a self-evident and unquestioned part of your daily life.

Regardless of what the circumstances and events of your life might be, you will begin to perceive a divine connection tying them all together. More and more, you will experience life as positive and joyful—not so much as a result of you making it that way as of you allowing it to become that way.

People will think and act in certain ways, and you will understand that it is actually God thinking and acting through them on your behalf. Various circumstances and conditions will develop in your life, and you will understand that God is orchestrating these developments. Events will transpire in your life, and you will understand that God is pulling the strings.

Much of the time you won't be able to recognize and know for sure which happenings are the products of divine intervention and which are not. In fact, much of the time things will transpire and you will never become aware that they even happened.

People will think and act due to divine intervention on your behalf, and you might never know it. Circumstances, conditions, and events will come about due to divine intervention on your behalf, and you might never be aware of their existence. Still, these things unseen and unknown by you will be fitting into the overall scheme of things. They will be working out as they need to in order for you to be able to live the life you and God have in mind for you.

At other times, though, the workings of divine intervention will be so extreme and obvious that you will not be able to miss them or deny them, even if you were inclined to do so. Such cases often occur during times of emergency, when a person's very life and physical wellbeing are at stake.

Chances are, you've had experiences of this sort. And you can read of the experiences of many others regarding this process of divine intervention. The basic theme is that an individual is at great risk of harm due to some health issue or other circumstance such as an automobile accident or near-drowning.

There are countless reports of spontaneous remission of cancer and other diseases and of some unseen force protecting a person from near-certain severe injury and even death by trauma, fire, human predators, and the list goes on and on. In instances such as these, the laws of the material world are often overridden, and what people can only describe as "miracles" transpire. If you need some reason to believe in the God Function, these many inspiring accounts should help to sway you toward that belief.

13
A Wake-Up Call

Whether or not God exists and what God might be should not be your concern at this time. Your concern at this time should be whether or not you *believe* God exists. Your concern should be what you *believe* God is. Your concern should be making the God Function, which appears to be a self-evident fact of creation, a recognized fact of your daily life.

Turn to God in everything, even in strengthening your belief in God if necessary. Pray to the very God you are striving to believe in, and the fact that you are praying to It will demonstrate and strengthen your belief in It. Do you want to make God real? Then do it. You have the power to make God real, just as God has the power to make you real.

Ask yourself this question: Can anything real and lasting exist outside of God? This is not so much a question to mentally ponder as it is a question to be answered through deep spiritual discernment.

You already know the truth, don't you? So why doubt yourself? Why doubt God? Go beyond your concept of God to the God Itself of which your concept is but a pale reflection. Is there actually a God beyond your concept of a God? You should no longer seriously consider the negative answer to that question if you want to keep the door open to the God you might have hoped and prayed would be your salvation.

Do not close the door to God. If you want to ensure the continued and expanding operation of the God Function in your life, one very effective way to do that is to keep the door open to God. If you have chosen to walk this God Function path as part of your spiritual and material journey, understand that the closer you are to God, the stronger your working connection with the God Function will be. Each breath you take brings you one step closer to the heart of God or moves you one step further away.

Remember, it's not so much about what God is as it is about what you think (believe) God is. If you can bring yourself to believe in the God that is what you have determined it should be, you will have taken hold of a powerful tool for working and reworking material reality and for designing and manifesting a life and a lifestyle few could conceive of.

Your God should be real, and your God should be here in this moment, ever present. God can give you the many worldly and spiritual gifts you long for, but there is one gift only you can give yourself. The one gift only you can give yourself is the gift of God Itself. God cannot—or at least *will* not—give you the gift of Itself. That would go against your inborn right to freedom of choice and spiritual free will.

In the end, even God must take a back seat and patiently wait for you to decide if and when It, God, will be allowed to come alive for you in a practical and observable way. Do you have any real concept of the extent of your power? You have the power to effectively keep God at bay, despite Its every attempt to gain your acceptance, trust, and cooperation.

And consider the possibility that it might actually be harder to not believe in God than it is to believe in God. Believing in God just might be the most natural, liberating, fruitful, and joyous thing you can do at this time in your life.

These words are not meant to convince you that God exists. These words are meant to get you to admit to yourself that you know God exists. Because if God is to exist—at least for you—your knowing it will be the catalyst that will make it a reality.

The words you are reading in this book are nothing if not a wake-up call. Listen. Can you hear it? God's alarm clock is ringing.

That God exists might be up for debate. What God is might be up for debate. But if you want God to be a part of your life, you should not participate in any debates about God. What others think and believe about God is not your concern. Your only concern is what *you* think and believe about God.

Make a stand, for or against God, and then live with it. Make a choice, for or against God, and then live with it. In the end, the choice is, in fact, yours, just as it always has been. If you choose to, you will be able to see a God that is at once both personal and impersonal. And if you choose to, you will see that God everywhere you look—even in a mirror.

14
A Life Transformed

Much of God's influence on your life through the medium of the God Function will be your rightful inheritance and reward in that, in one way or another, at one time or another, you have worked for it and earned it. Some or much of God's influence on your life might be as a result of Grace, meaning you have not worked for and earned it so much as God has freely bestowed it upon you as a divine gift.

But the question of whether you have earned God's favor or it has been given to you as a divine gift is not a question you need to be concerned with. It is beside the point. The point is that God continues to work for your highest best good by working on you directly and on the world at large on your behalf. The point is that God is and will be as real for you as you allow It to be. The point is that you are the keeper at your gate and always have been. The point is that unless you have already let God through your gate, God is patiently waiting for you to do so.

Now think about this: What do you want out of life? Better health? Better relationships? More worldly success? More opportunities for self-expression and sharing? Financial security? Peace of mind? To be safe? What do you really want out of life?

Know that you can have many of the things you want out of life and likely to a degree you have not yet imagined. And just how are you to go about the task of attaining many of the things you want out of life? The answer should be clear to you now.

You have now learned what the God Function is. You have now learned how the God Function works. You have now learned one very effective way to work the God Function. You have now learned how to live an inspired, charmed, and magical life.

That there is a mechanism in creation that acts as God is generally said and thought to act is self-evident. That mechanism is the God Function. It exists. It is perceivable through Its activity.

The God Function can give you everything you need. In fact, the God Function knows better than you what you need. The God Function can give you much of what you want. In fact, the God Function knows better than you what you want.

On some level, small or great, you have seen and recognized the God Function at work in the lives of others and in your own life as well. The truth of the God Function is self-evident. It needs no defending. Again, the God Function exists. The God Function is predictable. The God Function is dependable. The God Function works.

Your life will be transformed to the degree that you accept the validity of the God Function, invite it into your experience, and act in ways harmonious with how the God Function operates. This is not a complex process, so don't make it one.

This could not be much simpler: There is a mechanism in creation that acts as God is generally said and thought to act, and your job is to act as if that mechanism is God Itself and in a way that will help you to have what you deem a good life.

AFTERWORD

Thank you for reading this book. I hope you have enjoyed it. And I hope you will continue to benefit from having read it. I have benefited greatly from having read countless books over the years.

I began to find my first self-help, spiritual, and metaphysical books in my early twenties, not long after I moved from New Jersey to California to try to find my way in the world. Before that move, I had no idea such books even existed.

And honestly, were it not for such books and my intense desire to learn, to grow, and to improve myself and my circumstances, I would have gone down a completely different road in life—a road I would rather not even think about or imagine.

Who could deny the assertion that books can and do change lives? It is my mission to write some of those books that do indeed change lives. I want people's lives to be better because I lived and because I wrote.

There are reasons I came into this life, and writing is one of them. I am living the life I was meant to live, and it is my sincere desire that you will live the life you were meant to live.

Can I ask two favors of you? First, if you think this or any of my other books can help people in some of the ways they could use help, will you help spread the word about me and my writings? You could do that by loaning my books to others, giving my books as gifts, and by telling people about my books and about me. By doing these things, you will bless me beyond measure, and I truly believe you will bless others beyond measure as well.

Second, please consider writing an honest review for this book. Doing so will help other readers decide whether or not the book might be right for them. And keep in mind that a review does not have to be long. Even just a few words or a sentence or two could be sufficient. And if you do not feel inclined to write a review at all, you can simply click on a star rating to rate the book and still have your voice heard.

Finally, always remember, you are capable of so much more than you have ever imagined. Learn, believe, act, and persist. If you will do those four things, nothing will stop you from continuing to build a better and better life for yourself and for those you care about.

Peace & Plenty . . .

ABOUT THE AUTHOR

James Goi Jr., aka The Attract Money Guru™, is the best-selling author of the internationally published *How to Attract Money Using Mind Power*, a book that set a new standard for concise, no-nonsense, straight-to-the-point self-help books. First published in 2007, that game-changing book continues to transform lives around the world. And though it would be years before James would write new books, and even more years before he would publish new books, that first book set the tone for his writing career. The tagline for James as an author and publisher is Books to Awaken, Uplift, and Empower™. And James takes those words seriously, as is evident in every book he writes. James: is a relative recluse and spends most of his time alone; is an advanced mind-power practitioner, a natural-born astral traveler, and an experienced lucid dreamer; has had life-changing encounters with both angels and demons, and even sees some dead people; has been the grateful recipient of an inordinate amount of life-saving divine intervention; is a poet and songwriter; is a genuinely nice guy who cares about people and all forms of life; fasts regularly; is a sincere seeker of higher human health; is an objective observer, a persistent ponderer, and a deliberate deducer; and has a supple sense of heady humor.

STAY IN TOUCH WITH JAMES

If you are a sincere seeker of spiritual truth and/or a determined pursuer of material wealth and success, James could be the lifeline and the go-to resource you have been hoping to find. Step One, subscribe to James's free monthly *Mind Power & Money Ezine* here: jamesgoijr.com/subscriber-page.html. Step Two, connect with James online anywhere and everywhere you can find him. You can start here:

Facebook.com/JamesGoiJr
Facebook.com/JamesGoiJrPublicPage
Facbook.com/HowToAttractMoneyUsingMindPower
Twitter.com/JamesGoiJr
Linkedin.com/in/JamesGoiJr
Pinterest.com/JamesGoiJr
Youtube.com/JamesGoiJr
Instagram.com/JamesGoiJr
Goodreads.com/JamesGoiJr
jamesgoijr.tumblr.com

James' Amazon Author Page

A great resource to help you keep abreast of James's ever-expanding list of books is his author page at Amazon.com. There you will find all of his published writings and have easy access to them in the various editions in which they will be published.

Suggested for You

From time to time, James comes across products he thinks might be of interest to his readers, and he posts the links to those products on his website. To see what might be currently listed, visit that page here: jamesgoijr.com/suggested.html

SPECIAL ACKNOWLEDGEMENT

To Kathy Darlene Hunt, who has been my rock, my Light, my safety net, and my buffer since I was in my twenties. She rightfully shares in the credit for every book I've written, for the books I'm working on now, and for every single book I will ever write.

Kathy Darlene Hunt
Author of *A Child of the Light*
jamesgoijr.com/kdh.html

A FREE GIFT FOR YOU!

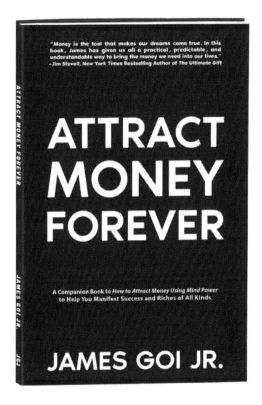

Attract Money Forever will deepen your understanding of metaphysics and mind-power principles as they relate to attracting money, manifesting abundance, and governing material reality. You'll learn how to use time-tested, time-honored, practical, and spiritual techniques to be more prosperous and improve your life in astounding and meaningful ways. Visit jamesgoijr.com/subscriber-page.html for your free download copy of this amazing book and to receive James's free monthly *Mind Power & Money Ezine*.

FURTHER READING

The 15-Minute Prayer Solution by Gary Jansen
Anatomy of the Sacred by James C. Livingston
Becoming God by Nancy J. Hudson
Born to Believe by Andrew Newberg M.D. and Mark
Robert Waldman
The Bushman Way of Tracking God by Bradford
Keeney, Ph.D.
The Cambridge Companion to Religious Studies by
Robert A. Orsi (Editor)
Can We Talk to God? by Ernest Holmes
Chicken Soup for the Soul: Answered Prayers by
Jack Canfield, Mark Victor Hansen and LeAnn
Thieman
Code Name God by Mani Bhaumik
The Constant Fire by Adam Frank
Contemporary Theories of Religion by Michael
Stausberg
Conversations with God by Neale Donald Walsch
The Cosmic Hologram by Jude Currivan
A Course in Miracles by Dr. Helen Schucman
Creating Miracles by Carolyn Godschild Miller Ph.D.
and Terry Lynn Taylor (Foreword)
Discovery of the Presence of God by David Hawkins
Divine Alignment by Squire Rushnell
Divine Guidance by Doreen Virtue
Divine Intervention by Daniel Fazzina
Divine Interventions by Dan Millman and Doug
Childers
Eight Theories of Religion by Daniel L. Pals
The Encyclopedia of God by Constance Victoria
Briggs
The Experience of God edited by Jonathan Robinson
Experiencing God by Henry T. Blackaby

Extraordinary Miracles in the Lives of Ordinary People by Therese Marszalek
The Faith Instinct by Nicholas Wade
The Favor of God by Jerry Savelle
Fingerprints of God by Barbara Bradley Hagerty
From Science to God by Peter Russell
The Genesis Code by Abraham Lopian
God: A Biography by Jack Miles
God: A Guide for the Perplexed by Keith Ward
God and the New Physics by Paul Davies
The God Code by Gregg Braden
The God Effect by Brian Clegg
The God Gene by Dean H. Hamer
God in the Equation by Corey S. Powell
The God in You by Prentice Mulford
God on a Harley by Joan Brady
The "God" Part of the Brain by Matthew Alper
The God-Shaped Brain by Timothy R. Jennings
God Stories by Jennifer Skiff
A God That Could Be Real by Nancy Ellen Abrams
The God Theory by Berhard Haisch
The God We Never Knew by Marcus J. Borg
God Within by Patti Conklin
The Golden Book of Melchizedek, Volume 1 by Dr. Joshua David Stone
The History of God by Karen Armstrong
The Holographic Universe by Michael Talbot
The Holy Science by Swami Sri Yukteswar
How God Changes Your Brain by Andrew Newberg, M.D. and Mark Robert Waldman
How to Believe in God by Clark Strand
How to Know God by Deepak Chopra
How to Know God's Will by Mark R. Moore
How to Let God Help You by Myrtle Fillmore
How You Can Be Led by the Spirit of God by Kenneth E. Hagin

Introducing Religion by Daniel L. Pals
Leave it to God by Christian D. Larson
Let God Fight Your Battles by Joyce Meyer
Living Fire and God's Law of Life by Hilton Hotema
Making Peace with God by Harold Bloomfield, M.D. and Philip Goldberg, Ph.D.
Miracles: 32 True Stories by Joanie Hileman
Miracles Are for Real by James L. Garlow and Keith Wall
Miracles Still Happen by Sheri Stone and Therese Marszalek
Modern-Day Miracles by Allison C. Restagno and Pastor Evans Barning (Foreword)
Mystical Mind by Eugene D'Aquili
Neuroscience and Religion edited by Volney P. Gay
The Neuroscience of Religious Experience by Patrick McNamara
Neuroscience, Psychology, and Religion by Malcolm Jeeves and Warren S. Brown
The Next Step by Patricia Diane Cota-Robles
On Being God by Carl Bozeman
On God by Jiddu Krishnamurti
Oneness by Rasha
Perceiving God by William P. Alston
The Perennial Philosophy by Aldous Huxley
The Power of I Am by Joel Osteen
The Power of Miracles by Joan Wester Anderson
The Power of Potential by Edwin Louis Cole
The Practice of the Presence of God by Brother Lawrence
Practicing the Presence by Joel S. Goldsmith
Prayer by Neville Goddard
Principles of Neurotheology by Andrew B. Newberg
Psychology and Religion by Andrew R. Fuller
Quantum Jumps by Cynthia Sue Larson
Quantum Theology by Diarmuid O'Murchu

Quiet Moments with God by Joseph Murphy
Religion by Malory Nye
Religious Experience Reconsidered by Ann Taves
Religious and Spiritual Experiences by Wesley J. Wildman
Religious Worlds by William E. Paden
Return to the One by Brian Hines
Sacred Pathways by Todd Murphy, His Holiness the Dalai Lama (Foreword), and Dr. Michael A. Persinger (Foreword)
The Secret of Working Knowingly with God by Walter Russell
The Science of God by Gerald L. Schroeder
The Science of Religion by Paramahansa Yogananda
Small Miracles by Yitta Halberstam, Judith Leventhal and Bernie S. Siegel (Preface)
Spiritual Harmony by Jerry Stocking
Stages of Faith by James W. Fowler
There Is a God in You by Parag and Diane Karkhanis
The Way of the Heart by Henri J.M. Nouwen
What God is Like by James Dillet Freeman
What Is God? by Jacob Needleham
What Is Self? by Bernadette Roberts
What the Buddha Taught by Walpola Rahula
What the Great Religions Believe by Joseph Gaer
When Science Meets Religion by Ian G. Barbour
Wholeness and the Implicate Order by David Bohm
Why Would Anyone Believe in God? by Justin L. Barrett
The Wisdom Within by Dr. Irving Oyle and Susan Jean
The Varieties of Religious Experience by William James
World Religions by Solomon A. Nigosian
You Can Talk with God by Edwin von Boltz

NOTES

NOTES

Made in United States
Orlando, FL
29 October 2024

53233086R00048